HOW TO OVERCOME TRAUMA

Reasons, Signs, Effects and freedom from a toxic relationship

Bertie Navarro

INTRODUCTION

Humans are social creatures. He needs to connect with the people around him in order to survive and remain content. The best feeling in the world is to love someone and to be loved. We refer to a relationship as the feeling of love and the connection between two people. Relationships with family, friends, acquaintances and romantic partners all play a significant role at some point in one's life. As a result, having a relationship is one of life's most important things.

In every person's life, having a relationship is very important. You need a relationship to stay happy, share your feelings, feel loved, have a connection, and better understand yourself. The relationship changes as you get older. As a result, a relationship can be defined as a bond between two people based on shared likes, needs, or love. Since birth, people go into a relationship. Actually there are generally four kinds of relationships:

Relationship to Family: The most fundamental kind of relationship is this one. It is born through blood, kinship, marriage, or even adoption. Family members like parents, grandparents, children, siblings, cousins, aunts, uncles and other relatives are typically included.

Friendship: A child begins to meet new people and attend school as he grows. It is during this time friendships are formed. The child makes friends based on what they like and doesn't like. At every stage, this relationship takes place. We do make new friends as we get older. However, friendship is a relationship that is reciprocal and is based on trust, care, and faith on both sides. Friendship is a unique gift from God that allows people to share a variety of resonant emotions with one another.

Close connection: Human has been dependably eager for affection. Most of the time, it's a relationship based on a strong sense of connection based on personality or physical characteristics. Typically, husband and wife share this bond. It is one of the most intimate and powerful relationships.

Acquaintances: Every day, we pass by a lot of people as we move across. They are not related or friends. They can be neighbors, a partner in crime, somebody you meet at the recreation area, or some other such individual. However, a relationship of this kind can develop into a friendship if it is treated with care and respect.

CHAPTER ONE

The most profound of these feelings are love and trust. Everyday interactions serve as the foundation for the development of relationships. The person must concentrate on the four fundamental characteristics in order to have a healthy relationship. They are love, trust, communication, and respect. The four pillars must be incorporated into the relationship's deep roots in order for it to thrive and last.

Communication between two people kicks off every relationship. To discuss issues and come up with a solution, it's important to have good communication. The relationship breaks down as a result of distrust and skepticism. Second, the foundation of any relationship is trust. Every relationship begins with family or friends; if trust is lacking, the relationship will eventually break down.

When you open up about how you really feel, you can earn each other's trust and loyalty. Respect is the third pillar. Respect is crucial in both the personal and professional spheres. Respect for oneself is reciprocated by respect for others. Respecting and caring for others builds a foundation for long-term relationships as well as self-respect. The latter is love. Care is the result of love. Love is something that everyone seeks in their lives. A loving relationship makes a person happy and strengthens the relationship.

Relationships do not develop overnight. They require constant attention and focus. People are more likely to remain content and happy when their relationships are healthy and successful. In addition, the standard of living rises. Investing in relationships can lead to "Happily Ever After," despite the fact that they may take time.

CHAPTER TWO

Whether you're just starting out as a single person or have been married for a long time, you'll be aware that there are advantages and disadvantages to both. Each relationship status has its own set of benefits and drawbacks, and depending on the circumstances, you may sometimes shift your feelings.

When it comes to our friendships, relationships, and other events in general, life typically has ups and downs that can affect how we feel about ourselves and others. If you're not sure if you're ready for a new relationship or if you're having mixed feelings about your current one, it might be time to weigh the benefits and drawbacks of each one.

Pro: There is always someone who is there for you. This is unquestionably an important reason to date someone. They will be there for you if you're in a good relationship. Whether it's online, when they text you every day and first like your Instagram posts, or when they physically cuddle you when you're having a bad day. You should be able to really relax with your boyfriend or girlfriend. It's unlike anything else in the world to have someone you can turn to for anything. Move on to the con!

Con: It's not as fun to go out with single friends as you think. Remember that great club night when you flirted your way into a VIP booth and Alex had an affair with a Raptor? It's possible that you're no longer up to fine-tuning the nightlife scene. You are much less motivated to go out, socialize, and flirt because you have responsibilities to your S/O.You already have a wonderful person whom you probably would rather spend time with than be groped in a damp, dark basement by a washed-up Degrassi cast member. Next is for the expert!

Pro: You are discovering a great deal about yourself, including what you want, what you don't want, and what you need in a partner. When you spend a lot of time with someone else, you'll figure out a few things like these. What do you require to feel at ease? Plenty of reassurance and communication? Loads of room? How do you know you are loved? Small presents? a second kiss before you say your goodbyes? Until someone shows you exactly what you deserve, you might not know what your standards are. or the things you don't, depending on whom you're dating. Move on to the con!

Con: With all of the pressures of work, maintaining a social life, and maintaining your sanity, you really do need to pencil in your relationship, despite how cliché that may sound. Make time for the people you want to see in your life, including your boyfriend, girlfriend, or the person you're seeing. Dislike having the arrangement to see your bae is especially hot, however, you ought to have a comprehension of dates and time spent together to abstain from tumbling off. Next for professionals

Pro: Reassurances about how cute, hot, and cool you are constantly, Hell ya. It's wonderful to hear this from someone other than your parents. Particularly on the off chance that you're not used to insistence from others. Obviously, you are aware that you are a target. Simply focus on yourself. However, hearing it from someone else is so wonderful. Even better on particularly unpleasant, gross, or who-is-that-in-the-mirror days. You absolutely do not require this assurance to maintain your mood, but it does not hurt Con: Someone who is accustomed to having such complete control over their own life might find the fact that you have someone to report back to a little strange. Not that your S/O is controlling by any means, however, you most certainly have had your portion of "Gracious poop, I haven't messaged _____ back in hours. "When you're dating, they'll probably want to know what you're up to, but it's easy to get distracted by the day's events and forget about your next game. It's just as annoying and frustrating when they quit their next game.

Pro: First dates, second dates, and all of the other nonsense that goes along with them are a thing of the past. You no longer have to deal with the ridiculous politics of dating. Would it be a good idea for you to text them first? Even though they last texted you 15 minutes ago, can you still message them? Put that in the past. You haven't heard from your S/O in several hours. That scumbag can be double-texted! When you spend time with someone for a long time as opposed to a short time, there is indefinitely less stress. You probably already said it, so you don't need to worry about sounding stupid. Surprisingly, they are still willing to sleep with you!

Con: You are aware that going out on a limb requires breaking up with your S/O. That adorable new receptionist is so sweet, and they also enjoy watching GOT and eating spicy tuna rolls. You are committed to your SO, even though you are aware that you would get along well together. Commitment alone accounts for half of a relationship. When you choose to go out with someone, you are choosing to be trustworthy and loyal, which means keeping many doors shut. If you want to date someone in your early 20s, you need to know that you'll meet a lot of people and feel more drawn to some of them than others.

Pro: Complete confidence in where you are at this moment In order to have healthy relationships, communication is essential. It is an incredible feeling to know that you and your significant other are content, relaxed, and together. You and they both know what you want, so you can just relax and enjoy each other's company. There is always a plus one, someone you can talk to and confide in. And to be sincere that is the greatest advantage of all.

CHAPTER THREE

What Is a Relationship That Is Harmful?

A relationship that makes you feel unsupported, misunderstood, denigrated, or attacked is considered toxic. When you're emotional, psychological, or physical well-being is threatened, a relationship is toxic.

A fundamentally unhealthy relationship can develop over time if it makes you feel worse rather than better. Almost any setting, from the playground to the boardroom to the bedroom, can have toxic relationships. You might even have to deal with toxic family relationships.

Because they are already sensitive to negative emotions, people with mental illnesses like bipolar disorder, major depression, or even depressive tendencies may be particularly susceptible to toxic relationships.

For instance, a person who suffers from bipolar disorder and is currently experiencing a mixed or depressive episode might be less able to maintain emotional stability than other people, which may eventually make that person an easier target for toxic people. However, toxic individuals can harm anyone.

What you need to know about toxic relationships, including how to tell if you're in one and what makes a relationship toxic. Additionally, you'll find advice on how to effectively manage these kinds of relationships.

How to Tell if a relationship is toxic Only you can tell if the bad things outweigh the good ones. However, if a person consistently poses a threat to your well-being through what they say, do, or do not do, the relationship is most likely toxic.

Connections that include physical or obnoxious attacks are most certainly delegated harmful. However, other, less obvious indicators of a toxic relationship include:

• You feel devalued and depleted because you give more than you receive.

• You feel disrespected on a consistent basis or that your needs are not being met.

• Over time, you notice a decline in your self-esteem.

• You feel alone, misunderstood, denigrated, or attacked.

• After speaking with the other person or being around them, you feel down, angry, or tired.

• You both bring the worst out of each other. You don't like it when, for instance, your competitive friend brings out a spiteful competitive streak in you.

• When you're around the person, you're not at your best. For instance, they seem to bring out a mean streak in you that you don't normally have, or they bring out the gossipy side of you.

• You feel as though you have to tread carefully around this person to avoid being stung by their venom.

• You attempt to cheer them up with a lot of energy and time.

• You're always at fault. They reverse events, making mistakes you thought were theirs suddenly fall on you.

How Does Love Bombing Work?

Relationships that are toxic versus abusive Relationships that are abusive, however, any relationship that is abusive can be considered toxic.

In most toxic relationships, boundaries are broken and respect is not respected. People sometimes engage in this behavior without even realizing it.

However, the relationship may be considered abusive if this kind of behavior is consistently displayed with the deliberate intention of causing harm to the other party.

There are many different kinds of abuse, including physical, emotional, and psychological abuse. The cycle of abuse is also often followed by abusive relationships.

For instance, the following are typically the stages of the abuse cycle: The tension begins to rise.

2. There is an abuse incident.

3. The perpetrator apologizes, assigns blame to the victim, or minimizes the abuse.

4. There is a time period when there is no abuse; be that as it may, the cycle in the long run rehashes.

Furthermore, it's possible that toxic relationships are more subjective than abusive ones. For instance, if you have a history of being duped, you might think that anyone who lies is bad for you; It's possible that someone else will be more receptive to letting it go and giving the person who lied another chance.

Toxic vs. Healthy Behavior When trying to figure out if a relationship is causing toxicity, it's important to look at the behaviors that occur most frequently.

To put it another way, if one or both of you are always selfish, mean, and disrespectful, it could be making the relationship toxic. However, if you are primarily supportive, understanding, and respectful, there may only be a few issues that contribute to toxicity that need to be addressed.

Whether you or the other person are showing signs of toxicity, it's critical to recognize them. The following are some indications of both harmful and healthy behaviors:

Healthy Behavior • Secure • Loving • Positive • Giving • Selfless • Encouraging • Uplifting • Trustworthy • Compassionate • Respectful Types of Toxic Relationships It is important to note that toxic relationships are not limited to romantic ones. Toxic behavior includes being insecure, jealous, negative, self-centered, critical, demeaning, disrespectful, and self-centered. They can be extremely stressful, particularly if the toxicity isn't effectively managed, and they exist in families, workplaces, and friendship groups.

• When negative behaviors occur: A toxic environment is created by some people's constant complaining, critical remarks, and general negativity. Perfectionism, unhealthy competitiveness, and frequent lying are all potentially harmful traits. Insecurities can also bring out the worst in people.

• When one or both individuals are unaware of themselves: Sometimes, people don't realize how bad they make other people feel. Additionally, it's possible that they are unaware of healthier means of communication. They probably don't understand how to read social cues well enough to know when they're annoying others or making them feel like they're being criticized or ignored.

• When someone intentionally causes harm to others: Some people intentionally act insensitive and rude. You might feel like you are the only one because of their mean words and actions in these situations. Toxic behavior includes the attempt to control or manipulate you.

• When a partner keeps cheating on you: A toxic element is added to the relationship when an intimate partner lies and cheats without even attempting to change their behavior.

• When someone abuses you: People's actions can be deemed abusive if they repeatedly and purposefully harm you. Abuse is never acceptable, regardless of whether they are verbally or physically abusing you.

Relationships that are toxic and drug addiction Someone who abuses drugs or alcohol may engage in toxic behaviors. They may be able to overcome their toxic characteristics with treatment; However, it's possible that relationships that were hurt by their addiction won't be completely restored.

You might want to reevaluate the unhealthy relationships in your life if any of the aforementioned scenarios apply to your situation.

How Bad Relationships Impact Your Health Narcissists and Sociopaths Some people, particularly narcissists and sociopaths, have a tendency to thrive on the admiration and attention of other people. In their quest for superiority, narcissists feel the need to outdo others and make them feel "less than."

If you share an accomplishment of which you are proud, they may purposely degrade you in subtle ways or make small remarks about you. They might also try to keep you guessing about whether or not they'll be nice to you every day. Alternatively, they might gaslight on a regular basis.

Because they truly believe that they never make mistakes, narcissists are known for not admitting when they make mistakes. In fact, they find it personally perilous to believe that they are not perfect.

While managing harmful, self-absorbed individuals, it's not generally clear whether they're mindful of what they are doing. But if their behavior consistently makes you feel bad about yourself, you'll need to get away from this person or at least accept that if they have to be in your life, remember that you need to be on your guard.

They won't be changed by this behavior change, but it can help alleviate some of the stress of dealing with them. Protecting yourself from the emotional abuse you receive when interacting with them is crucial:

• Remind yourself that you won't be able to change them, and confronting them may only elicit more resentment without bringing about any change.

• Maintain your distance from them.

• Recognize that if the person needs to be in your life, you need to be on your guard.

How to Tell if a coworker has malignant narcissism Coworkers: If it's a coworker and their proximity is a problem, you might want to move your desk. For instance:

If the person comes to you to complain, you could try referring them to a manager, after which you could calmly go back to work. Before they realize it, you may need to repeat this a lot.

It will likely be more challenging when dealing with family and friends because there may not be an easy way to get rid of the toxic person from your life.

If you have a friend who is very bad for you, you might just need to spend less time with them .If you're worried about offending them, spread out your visits over a longer period of time to make it less obvious (though they might still notice).

When the toxic individual is a close friend or member of the family, it may also be possible to encourage them to attend therapy, which is frequently required to address the toxicity's root cause.

CHAPTER FOUR

Is it necessary for you to leave your toxic marriage?

Effects of Toxic Relationships Your self-esteem, mental health, and physical health may be seriously harmed by toxic relationships.

A toxic relationship may make it harder for you to take care of yourself because of the constant drama in the relationship. This can cause us to lose focus on the other relationships in our lives and cause us to feel socially isolated, which can lead to other problems like depression or poorer quality of sleep2. If you're constantly dealing with a tumultuous or toxic person or relationship, you might have to give up your normal routine, which might include things like exercise, personal hygiene, hobbies, and other things. Over time, this sacrifice may result in the deterioration of mental and physical health as a whole.

Relationship Toxicology and Mental Health According to one study, unhealthy relationships can actually make anxiety and stress disorders worse. However, a 2016 University of Michigan study found that "stress and [negative] relationship quality directly affects the cardiovascular system."3 Healthy relationships can actually improve these conditions."4 Over time, all of these things hurt your health and may even cause you to develop unhealthy ways of coping, like drinking or eating when you're sad.

Managing Toxic Relationships Although it is not possible to avoid all toxic relationships, particularly those with coworkers or family members, they can be managed with self-care, awareness, and healthy boundaries.

If you're in a toxic relationship where you bring out the worst in each other or fail to bring out the best in each other, you might want to work on fixing the relationship and changing the dynamic, especially if the relationship has other advantages.

When you're both willing to make changes, assertive communication and healthier boundaries are frequently the keys to bringing out the best in one another.

A few additional steps for dealing with a toxic relationship are as follows:

• Talk about what you're seeing with the other person. Take responsibility for your part in the situation and be assertive about your needs and feelings.

• Decide together if you want to alter the dynamic to ensure that both of your needs are met after discussing the issue you see.

• Reassess your relationship and consider the following questions: Is this person seriously affecting your mental health and self-esteem?

• Avoid spending too much time with people who make you unhappy or frustrated. You might need to limit your interactions with this person if they are someone you need to interact with, like a family member or a coworker.

• When describing your feelings and emotions, use "I feel" statements if you decide to discuss your concerns. They won't feel as defensive as they would otherwise.

• Recognize that some toxic people simply refuse to change, particularly those who lack social skills or self-awareness.

• When the situation calls for it, make an effort to defend you without engaging in confrontation.

How to Get Out of a Dangerous Relationship If you've tried to set boundaries but the other person doesn't respect them, it might be time to break up. However it tends to be trying to do as such, recollect that the main thing is focusing on yourself, your requirements, and your well-being.

The way you decide to end the relationship depends on how safe you feel and the circumstances. You might:

• Specify the reasons for your decision to end the relationship and tell the person directly.

• Allow the relationship to end over time by communicating less and less with this person.

• Stop talking right away, especially if a relationship is putting your safety at risk.

You can try to avoid blaming the other person or becoming defensive if you choose to talk to them directly and take responsibility for your emotions. In the end, you have no control over how they react, but you can try to use strategies to keep the conversation from getting out of hand.

In order to safely leave a romantic relationship, you may need to build a support network. For instance, you might decide to talk to the person in a public setting if you are worried about how they will react. Make arrangements to meet up with a trusted person after the fact by informing them of the time and location of this event.

Until you find a new place to live away from your partner, you might have to live with a friend or family member.

CHAPTER FIVE

CONCLUSION

A Word from Very well: It's important to focus on your health and well-being when dealing with any toxic relationship. As a result, if you're dealing with someone who makes you unhappy and drained of energy, you should think about cutting them out of your life or at the very least limiting the amount of time you spend with them. Additionally, seek immediate assistance if you are the victim of emotional or physical abuse.